Seahorses

by Sylvia M. James

Photo Credits:
Front cover: © Gibbs, M. OSF/Animals Animals; back cover: © K. B. Sandved/Photo Researchers, Inc.; pp. 1, 3: © OSF/Animals Animals; p. 4 (top left): © Dani/Jeske/Animals Animals; p. 4 (bottom left): © Steven David Miller/Animals Animals; pp. 4 (top right), 7 (Long-snouted): © W. Gregory Brown/Animals Animals; p. 4 (bottom right): © Marian Bacon /Animals Animals; pp. 5, 6 (Spotted): © Mike Severns/Tom Stack & Associates, Inc.; pp. 6 (Barbour's), 7 (Crowned, Dwarf, Knysna), 8 (top right), 10 (inset), 12 (inset), 13 (inset), 14 (inset), 17 (inset), 19 (inset): George Grall, © National Aquarium in Baltimore; p. 6 (Pygmy): © Carlos Villoch; pp. 6 (Giant Pacific), 8 (left): © Miriam Agron /Animals Animals; pp. 6 (White's), 8 (bottom right): © Fritz Prenzel/Animals Animals; p. 6 (Tiger-tail): © Mark Strickland/Seapics.com; p. 7 (Thorny): © Fred Bavendam/Minden Pictures; pp. 7 (Lined), 11 (left), 17, 23: © Zig Leszczynski/Animals Animals; p. 7 (Pot-belly): © Brian Parker/Tom Stack & Associates, Inc.; p. 9 (top): © James D. Watt Photography; p. 9 (bottom): © Atkinson, K. OSF/Animals Animals; pp. 12, 14, 15: © Tom & Therisa Stack/Tom Stack & Associates, Inc.; p. 13: © Fritz Prenzel/Animals Animals; p. 16: © Breck P. Kent/Animals Animals; p. 18: © C. V. Angelo/ Photo Researchers; p. 19 (top left): © Carl Roessler/Animals Animals; p. 19 (bottom left): © John C. Stevenson/Animals Animals; p. 19 (top right): © Norbert Wu/Norbert Wu Productions; pp. 20, 22: © Rudie Kuiter/Seapics.com; pp. 21, 24 (full page): © Kuiter, R. OSF/Animals Animals; p. 24 (inset): © George Grall/National Geographic.

Illustrated map on page 10 copyright © by C.R.E.E. Alain Salesse Enr. under exclusive license to MONDO Publishing.
Text copyright © by Sylvia M. James

For information contact:
MONDO Publishing
980 Avenue of the Americas
New York, NY 10018
Visit our website at www.mondopub.com

Printed in Guangzhou, China
Nordica International Ltd., 12362

ISBN 978-1-59034-034-9

Designed by Annette Cyr

Library of Congress Cataloging-in-Publication Data

James, Sylvia M.
    Seahorses / Sylvia M. James
        p. cm.
    Summary: Photographs and simple text show what a sea horse is, its physical characteristics, and how it reproduces.
    ISBN 1-59034-034-5 (pbk.)
    1. Sea horses--Juvenile literature. [1. Sea horses.] I. Title

QL638.S9 J34
597'.6798--dc21

2001054407

Contents

What Is a Seahorse?..................4

Parts of a Seahorse's Body......12

Baby Seahorses..................20

What Is a Seahorse?

There are many kinds of fish.

The seahorse is a kind of fish.

There are about 32 kinds of seahorses.
Here are some of them.

Pygmy Seahorse

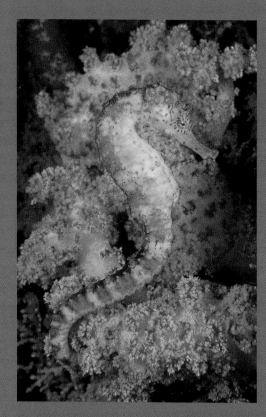

Tiger-tail Seahorse

Giant Pacific Seahorse

Spotted Seahorse

Barbour's Seahorse

White's Seahorse

Long-snouted Seahorse

Thorny Seahorse

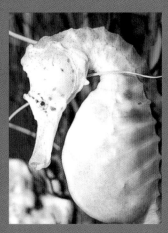

Pot-belly Seahorse

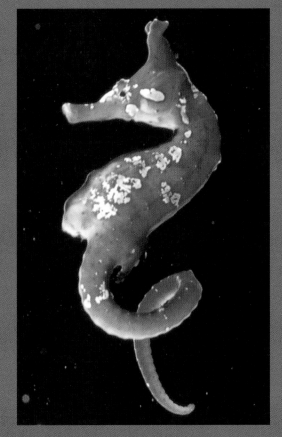

Crowned Seahorse

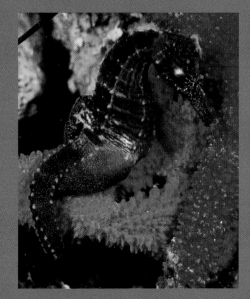

Lined Seahorse

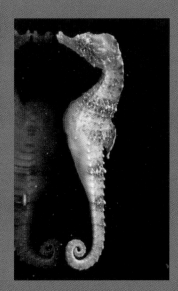

Knysna Seahorse

Dwarf Seahorse

7

Seahorses are many different sizes.

Dwarf Seahorse
1.5 inches (3.8 cm)

Giant Pacific Seahorse
12 inches (30.5 cm)

White's Seahorse
5 inches (12.7 cm)

Some are as small as grapes.

Pygmy Seahorse
.75 inch (2 cm)

Some are as big as bananas.

Pot-belly Seahorse
12 inches (30.5 cm)

Seahorses live in warm shallow water.

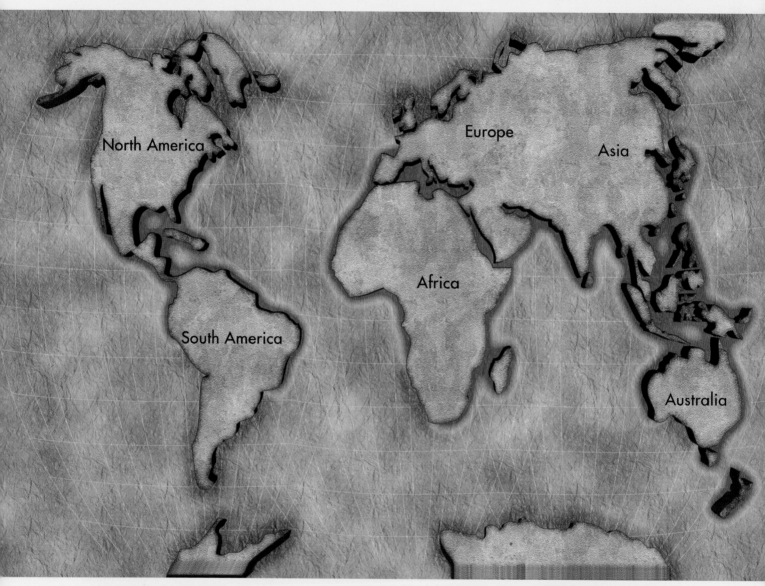

North America

Europe

Asia

South America

Africa

Australia

The yellow area shows where seahorses live.

Seahorses can live up to four years.

Seahorses live only in saltwater.

Parts of a Seahorse's Body

A seahorse has a long snout.

A seahorse's mouth is at the end of its snout.

snout _____

mouth _____

A seahorse sucks up food with its long snout.

The seahorse uses its snout like a straw.

A seahorse has one eye on each side of its head.

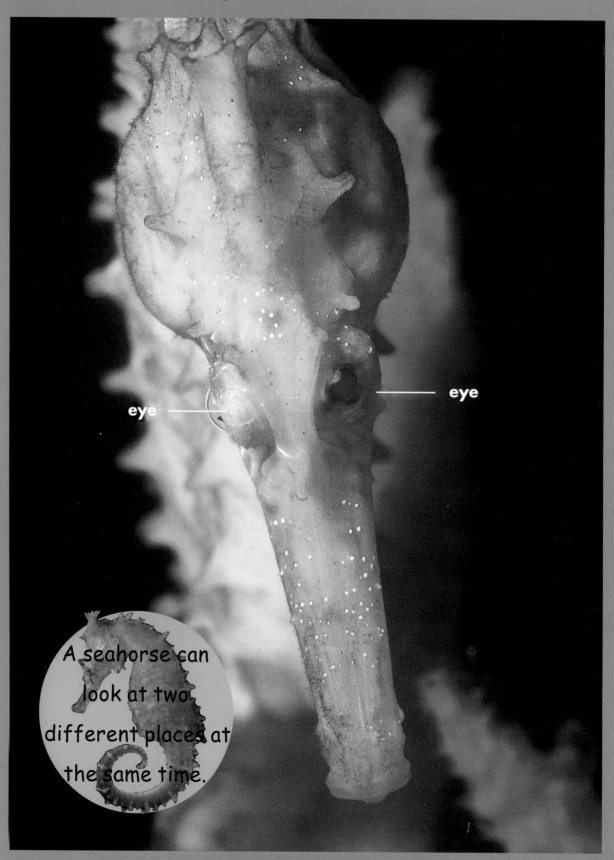

eye ——————————— eye

A seahorse can look at two different places at the same time.

A seahorse does not have teeth.

mouth ──────

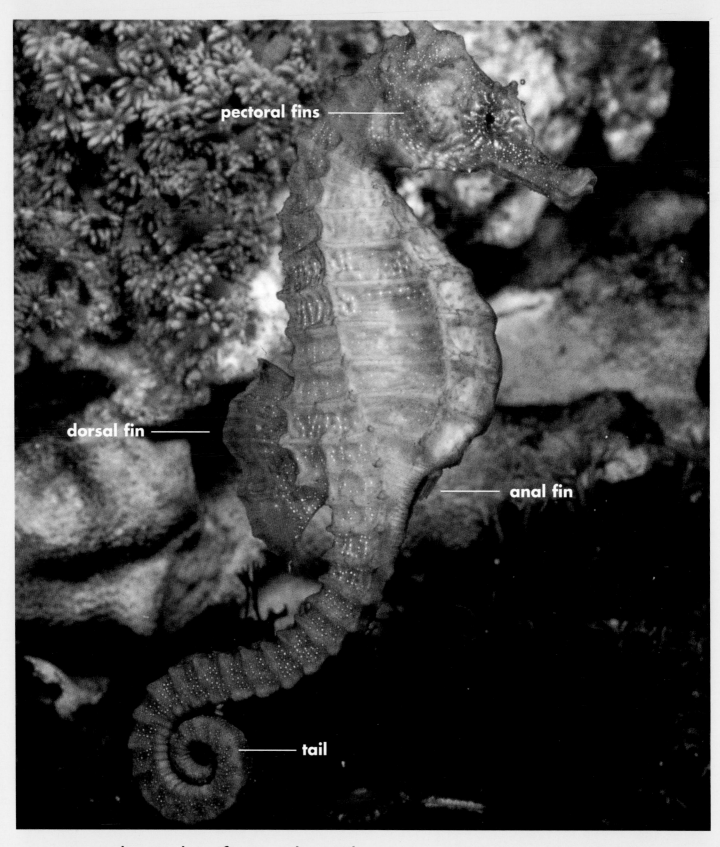

pectoral fins

dorsal fin

anal fin

tail

A seahorse has fins and a tail.

A seahorse swims by moving its back fin.

A seahorse's back fin moves faster than a person's eye can see.

A seahorse curls its tail around things to stay in one place.

Some seahorses can change color.

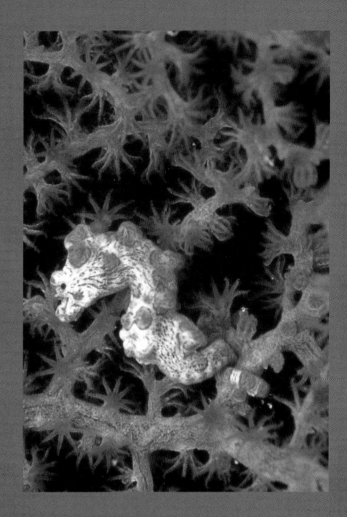

By changing color to match what's around them, seahorses can hide from enemies.

Baby Seahorses

A seahorse has many babies at one time.

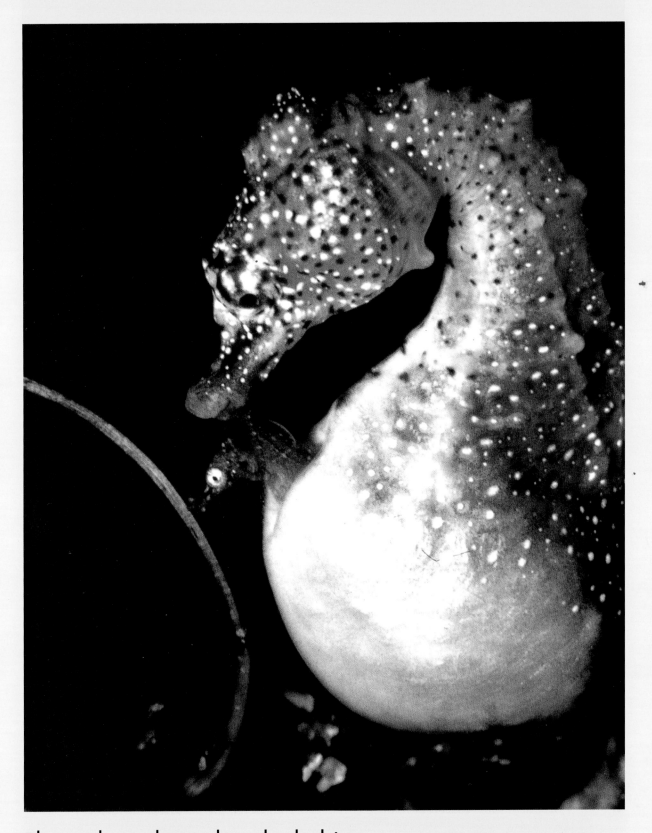

The male seahorse has the babies.

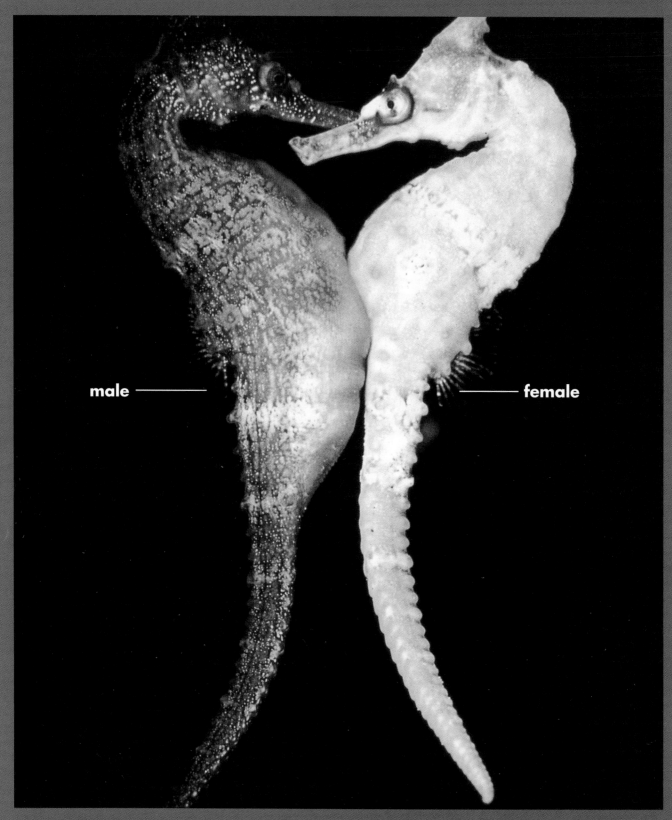

male ——— ——— female

The female seahorse puts her eggs in the male seahorse's pouch.

pouch

The male's pouch gets bigger as the babies grow.

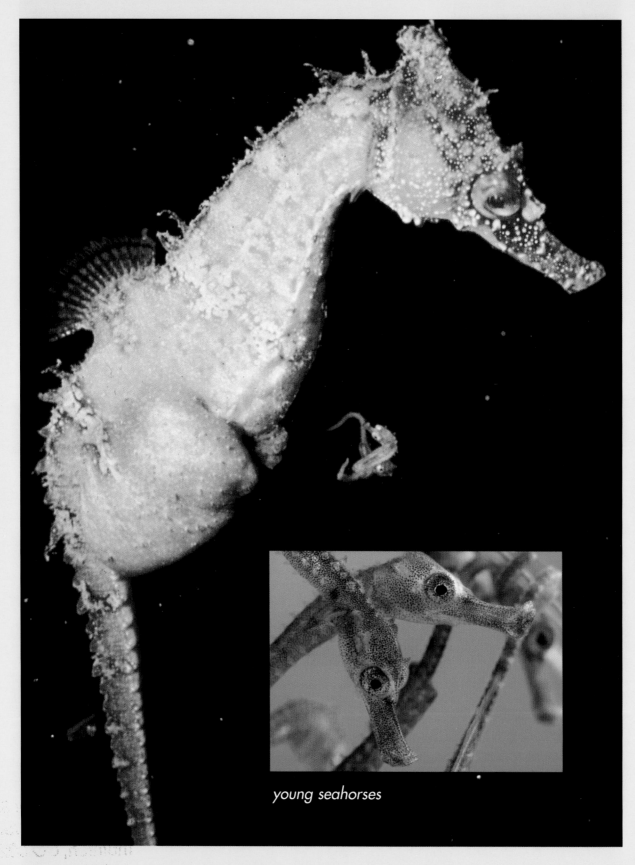

young seahorses

The babies swim out of the pouch when they are born.